Private Practice Blueprint® 101

How to Start a Private Practice from Scratch

Janessa M. Borges, LCSW

Janessa Borges, LCSW

Private Practice Blueprint® 101: How to Start a Private Practice from Scratch

Copyright © 2025 Janessa Borges

All rights reserved.

No part of this book may be reproduced, stored in a retrieval system, or transmitted in any form or by any means—electronic, mechanical, photocopying, recording, or otherwise—without the prior written permission of the publisher, except for brief quotations used in reviews, articles, or educational content with proper attribution.

This book is intended solely for informational and educational purposes. It reflects the personal opinions, insights, and experiences of the author and is not intended to serve as a substitute for legal, financial, accounting, or professional business advice.

While the author is a licensed therapist, she is not an attorney, accountant, or financial advisor. The information provided in this book does not constitute legal or tax advice, nor does it replace the guidance of licensed professionals. Readers should consult with a qualified attorney, certified public accountant (CPA), or other relevant professional before making any decisions regarding business formation, taxes, or compliance.

Published by Latinas Empowering Latinas LLC
Naples, FL
https://www.janessaborges.com/

ISBN: 979-8-9926530-8-3

Cover Design by Janessa Borges
Interior Layout by Janessa Borges

Printed in the United States of America

First Edition: 2025

For permissions, bulk purchases, or media inquiries, contact: janessamborges@gmail.com

Table of Contents

Chapter 1: Key Decisions   13

    Lesson 1: Naming Your Business   17

    Lesson 2: Deciding on Your Business Structure   27

    Lesson 3: Office Space   37

    Lesson 4: In-Network or Out-of-Network   51

Chapter 2: Foundations 101   71

    Lesson 1: Glossary of Private Practice Terms   71

    Lesson 2: Private Practice Requirement Checklist   81

Chapter 3: Administration of Private Practice   89

    Lesson 1: Startup Costs of Private Practice   89

    Lesson 2: Initial Paperwork   97

    Lesson 3: Everything Admin—Building a Strong Foundation   109

    Lesson 4: Billing Made Simple   117

    Lesson 5: Mastering Invoices & Superbills   125

What's Next!   131

Janessa Borges, LCSW

Welcome

Congratulations! I'm thrilled you're here, and I can't wait for you to dive into *Private Practice Blueprint® 101*. This book is the culmination of years of experience, meticulous planning, and an unwavering passion to help clinicians, like you, turn their dreams into reality.

Together, we'll cover everything you can imagine—and some things you probably haven't even thought of yet—to get you fully prepared to open the doors to your own private practice.

So, take a deep breath and get ready. I'm sending you all my encouragement and know that I'm rooting for you every step of the way. My hope is that this book exceeds your expectations, equips you with everything you need to get your doors open, and inspires you to create the life and career you've been dreaming of.

Janessa Borges, LCSW

Introduction

I'm so excited you're here because I wholeheartedly believe moments like this—when you take a leap of faith—are transformative. This is your time, and I'm here to remind you that you are exactly where you're meant to be.

My mission is simple: to empower clinicians like you to believe in your capability and worthiness so that you succeed in private practice. You deserve a life you love, one where your career aligns with your purpose and your dreams. If you're here, I imagine you're not quite in that place yet—but I'm confident that if you commit to these lessons, embrace the process, and give yourself the time and space to do the work, you will create the practice and life you envision.

Before we begin, let me share a bit about myself. I was born and raised in Miami to Cuban immigrants who sacrificed so much for their family. From them, I learned to be grateful, strong, respectful, loyal, and brave. Most importantly, they instilled in me the belief that I could achieve anything I set my mind and heart to.

I hold degrees in psychology, criminal justice, and social work, and I earned my clinical graduate degree from the Ivy League at New York University in the heart of Greenwich Village. My journey includes graduating with honors, receiving academic and community service scholarships, and a nearly two-decade career in mental health. For over 10 years, I've owned and operated my private practice, and I'm licensed as a mental health therapist in both New Jersey and Florida.

Today, I'm here as your mentor, business strategist, mindset coach, and biggest cheerleader. My goal is to share what I've learned, show you what's possible, and guide you toward creating a life you love.

This book is your roadmap, and I'm walking this journey with you. It's been broken into weekly bite-sized lessons designed to give you clarity and confidence at every step. I encourage you to make the investment in your time and, most importantly, in yourself. Your dream of opening a private practice is within reach, and it has the potential to change your life on every level.

Janessa Borges, LCSW

How to Get the Most Out of This Book

I know how busy life can be—whether you're juggling your roles as a parent, clinician, partner, or entrepreneur.

To support you along the way, I've created extra resources and tips based on my personal journey. These tools have been instrumental in my success, and I know they'll help you too.

I meticulously laid out the order of this book to follow the process you need to have a smooth transition into private practice. I know first hand how tempting it could be to jump ahead, but I encourage you to go through the book in order. There's a method to my madness.

Remember, success isn't just about reading, it's about doing the work, taking action, and committing to the process. Your dream practice and your ideal life are waiting for you—so let's get started.

Janessa Borges, LCSW

Chapter 1: Key Decisions

Introduction

Welcome! I'm so excited you're here. This book has been a long time in the making, and I've designed it to guide you strategically and efficiently toward building your private practice. My goal is to save you time, money, and frustration while equipping you with the tools to succeed.

Module 1 is all about key decisions — the foundational choices that will set the tone for your journey. These are not the conventional checklists you might be expecting, but I promise they're essential for your success. The decisions you make here will serve as the cornerstone of your practice.

Here's what we'll cover:

1. Deciding on your business name — A seemingly simple step that often trips up even the most seasoned entrepreneurs.
2. Choosing your business structure — While not the most exciting topic, it's a critical decision that requires careful thought.
3. Selecting your space or virtual platform — Whether physical or virtual, this choice has significant implications.
4. Insurance paneling or out-of-network — My personal favorite topic, as it's one of the most impactful decisions you'll make for your practice.

Each lesson will provide you with the pros, cons, and key considerations you need in order to make informed choices. Along the way, I'll share insights and stories from my own journey to help you navigate yours. These decisions might not be what you were expecting, but trust me, they are essential.

They'll shape the structure and soul of your practice and set you up for long-term success. Let's dive in and get started!

Janessa Borges, LCSW

Lesson 1: Naming Your Business

"If you don't know where you're going, you'll wind up somewhere else."

—Yogi Berra

This quote is one of my favorites, because it perfectly captures the importance of starting with intention. Your business name is more than a label—it's the banner under which your dreams will fly. It reflects your mission, your vision, and the community you wish to serve.

This perfectly encapsulates why starting with your business name is so important. Your business name is more than just a label; it's the first step in creating a vision for your practice.

Why Your Business Name Matters

Your business name is foundational. It will appear on legal documents, your bank accounts, marketing materials, and more. It sets the tone for how clients perceive you and can influence your brand's longevity. Let's explore two common approaches to naming your business.

Option 1: Using Your Name

Many therapists choose to name their business after themselves. This approach is straightforward, timeless, and often aligns with the personal nature of our work. Many therapists choose their own name for simplicity. After all, *you* are the cornerstone of your practice. Here are some pros to consider:

Pros:

- Simplicity: Clients easily associate your name with your services. It's easy to remember and straightforward to set up.
- Brand Consistency: Your name becomes synonymous with your expertise. Your name remains a constant, even if you expand into other ventures like books, workshops, or products.
- Recognition & Long-term Value: If you're the constant in your business, your name will always be relevant. Your name becomes synonymous with the value you provide.

However, there are also considerations to keep in mind, especially around privacy. As clinicians, confidentiality is paramount—not just for clients, but for ourselves and our families. Using your name might blur those lines, particularly in the digital age, where a quick search can reveal more than you'd like.

When I started, I was still using my maiden name. It was a deliberate choice, rooted in pride for the sacrifices my parents and I made for my Ivy League education. My maiden name became a tribute to the legacy I was building. Later, after I was married and had children, I appreciated this separation between my professional and personal life. It allowed me to honor my roots while maintaining a layer of privacy for my family.

Cons:

- Privacy: Using your name may raise concerns about confidentiality for you and your family.
- Scalability: If you plan to expand your practice or bring on other clinicians, your name may limit your branding options.

If you choose this route but have privacy concerns, consider using your maiden name or a variation of your name.

Option 2: Creating a Company Name

If you dream of a practice that grows beyond yourself—maybe with a team of clinicians or additional services—a business name might be a better fit. A company name can convey your vision and align with your long-term goals.

Here's how to approach this decision:

Start with Your Why: Why did you choose this path? What impact do you want to make? Your answers will guide you toward a name that feels authentic and inspiring.

Research Thoroughly: Check your state's business registry to ensure the name isn't already taken. Don't stop there—Google it, too. Sometimes, names aren't legally registered but are in active use, or worse, have a negative association. I learned this the hard way. I once fell in love with a name for my second business. It was perfect—or so I thought. After some research, I discovered it had been tied to a platform I definitely did not want to be associated with.

Needless to say, I moved on. It's a reminder not only to follow your passion but also to do your homework.

Be Flexible: If the name you want is taken, play around with variations. When I couldn't secure "Oceanside Wellness" for my practice, I worked with an attorney to brainstorm alternatives. With creativity and persistence, I landed on a name that felt just as meaningful.

Alternatively, you can create a unique company name that reflects your vision and values. This option allows for more creativity and flexibility, especially if you plan to grow your practice beyond yourself.

Pros:

- Branding Opportunities: A creative name can communicate your mission and attract your ideal clients.
- Scalability: A company name gives you room to grow and expand your services.

Cons:

- Availability: Ensure your desired name isn't already in use or trademarked. Check your state's business registry and perform a Google search.
- Connotations: Research the name to avoid negative associations. For instance, I once considered a name that seemed perfect until I discovered it was previously associated with an inappropriate platform. Needless to say, I moved on.

Tips for Choosing Your Business Name

1. Anchor it to Your "Why": Reflect on why you're starting your practice and what you want to achieve.
2. Do Your Homework: Check for availability and potential trademarks.
3. Think Long-term: Consider how the name aligns with your future goals.
4. Get Feedback: Share your ideas with trusted colleagues or mentors to get their perspective.
5. Be Flexible: If your first choice isn't available, play around with variations or synonyms.

When I named my practice, I initially envisioned the show "Private Practice." I'm a huge fan of Shonda Rhimes and her shows. I loved the idea of having a "one stop shop" of wellness that offered not just mental health services, but other types of "Self-care" practices—I was thinking yoga, reiki, acupuncture, all the things that conventional medicine didn't always offer—keeping in mind a person's entire wellness, and any modality that would provide proactive care, stress relief and develop a holistic treatment process.

My dream was to have my very own "Oceanside Wellness." Unfortunately, the name was already registered as an entity in my state. After some brainstorming and consultation, I landed on an alternative name that still felt authentic and aligned with my vision. The process took time, but it was worth it.

Final Thoughts

Your business name is your first big decision, but it's just the beginning of your journey. Take your time, trust the process, and remember that every step brings you closer to the practice you've been dreaming of.

Janessa Borges, LCSW

Lesson 2: Deciding on Your Business Structure

In this lesson, we're diving into an essential topic: deciding on your business structure. This is the foundation of everything else you'll do—your taxes, your legal protections, your finances—so it's a big step. But don't worry; I'll walk you through it step by step.

Before we begin, let me say this: you're here because you're ready to make your dreams a reality. You're ready to build something for yourself, something that aligns with your goals and values. This step may feel overwhelming, but I want you to know that you've got this. You don't have to know it all today. Keep going, because all of this hard work will pay off.

Now, a quick disclaimer: I am not an attorney, a tax professional, or a legal advisor. Everything I'm sharing with you in this lesson is for educational purposes only. I strongly encourage you to consult professionals—your attorney, accountant, or legal advisor—before making final decisions. This lesson is your starting point, not your final destination.

What is a Business Structure, and Why Does it Matter?

Your business structure determines how your practice operates, how you pay taxes, and how much legal protection you have. It's the framework for your private practice. Choosing the right structure can save you time, money, and stress down the road. It's an important decision, but one you can change later as your practice evolves.

So, let's get started by breaking down your options.

Option 1: Sole Proprietorship

A sole proprietorship is the simplest and most straightforward option. It's quick to establish, requires minimal paperwork, and is inexpensive. It's ideal if you're just starting out and testing the waters, especially if you're not yet earning significant income. In this structure, you're the sole owner of your practice, and you're responsible for everything.

However, as a sole proprietor, there's no legal separation between you and your business. You and your business are considered one entity. This means:

- All income, expenses, and liabilities are yours. This can make taxes simple, but it puts a lot of responsibility on your shoulders.

- No legal protection. If someone sues your business, your personal assets—your house, car, savings—are at risk.

If you decide to start as a sole proprietor, you'll need to research the forms required in your city, county, or state. Deadlines and fees vary, so make sure you know what's expected in your area.

Option 2: Limited Liability Company (LLC)

An LLC, or Limited Liability Company, is one of the most popular choices for clinicians. It's relatively simple to set up and maintain, while providing significant legal and financial protections.

Here's what you need to know about an LLC:

- Separation of assets: Your personal and business assets are legally distinct,

protecting your personal finances from business debts or lawsuits.
- Simple setup and maintenance: It doesn't require as much paperwork or expense as a corporation.
- Flexible ownership: An LLC can have one owner (you) or multiple owners.

This structure is a great choice for those who want peace of mind as they grow their practice.

Option 3: Professional Limited Liability Company (PLLC)

A PLLC is similar to an LLC but specifically designed for licensed professionals like therapists, doctors, and attorneys. In some states, you're required to use a PLLC instead of an LLC due to the nature of your work. It depends on your state and licensing board, so *always, always, always* do your due diligence. Requirements are always changing and you want to make sure you're following the rules so that you don't jeopardize your license. Keep in mind that not every state offers this option, so be sure to check your state's regulations.

Like an LLC, a PLLC provides legal separation between you and your business, offering protection for your personal assets.

Option 4: S-Corporation (S-Corp)

An S-Corp is a tax designation, not a business entity. You can establish an LLC and later choose to be taxed as an S-Corp. This is often recommended for businesses that are earning significant profits (usually over $60,000 annually).

Here's what to consider:

- Tax benefits: Being taxed as an S-Corp can save you money on self-employment

taxes. Instead of paying taxes on your entire income, you'll pay yourself a salary and only pay self-employment taxes on that amount. The rest of your income is taxed as a distribution, which has a lower rate.
- Additional responsibilities: You'll need a bookkeeper, an accountant, and you'll file taxes quarterly instead of annually. This adds to your administrative workload and costs.

If you're just starting out, this may not be the best option. However, it's worth revisiting once your practice is more established.

Option 5: C-Corporation (C-Corp)

A C-Corp is a more complex and formal business structure. It's typically used by larger businesses or those with plans to sell the company in the future.

Here's what you need to know:

- Separate legal entity: Like an LLC, a C-Corp offers strong legal protections.
- Double taxation: C-Corps pay taxes on their profits, and owners pay taxes again on dividends. This can make them less appealing for smaller businesses.
- High costs and paperwork: Setting up and maintaining a C-Corp is expensive and time-consuming.

Unless your long-term goal is to sell your private practice, a C-Corp likely isn't necessary.

Important Tax Notes

No matter which structure you choose, you'll need to stay on top of tax deadlines:
- Sole Proprietorships and LLCs: File taxes by April 15 for both federal and state (if applicable).

- S-Corps and C-Corp: File quarterly taxes. This requires meticulous record-keeping and planning.

In addition, some cities or counties may have local business taxes. These vary widely, so be sure to research what applies in your area.

Your Next Steps

Now that we've covered the basics, here's what I recommend:

1. Research your state's requirements: Look into the forms, fees, and deadlines for your chosen structure. Start with your state's Department of Revenue or Secretary of State website.
2. Consult with professionals: Reach out to an attorney or accountant to ensure you're making the right decision for your specific situation.

3. Decide and commit: Once you've chosen your business structure, finalize it. Celebrate this milestone—one more step toward making your dream a reality!

Resources to Support You

I've recorded podcast episodes with my favorite legal experts for entrepreneurs. Head over to janessaborges.com/podcast to access them for free.

Final Thoughts

Take the time to get this right, and you'll thank yourself later. Do your research, make an informed decision, and move forward with confidence. You've got this.

Lesson 3: Office Space

In this lesson, you'll learn what options you have when you're starting your practice, the pros and cons of each, and decide what works best for you.

Option 1: Virtual Therapy

Let's start with virtual therapy, especially given the increasing demand for flexibility and accessibility. This option became a lifeline during the pandemic and remains a viable, cost-effective choice for many. Virtual therapy offers unparalleled convenience for clients with health concerns, transportation challenges, or geographical limitations. Think about those snowy mornings, rainy afternoons, or tropical storms here in Florida—it allows sessions to continue without cancellations.

Virtual therapy also minimizes overhead costs, but there are essential considerations:

- Licensing: Ensure you're licensed in the state where your client resides. While temporary exceptions were made during the pandemic, compliance is critical.
- Confidentiality: Verify that both you and your clients have secure, private spaces to conduct sessions. For clients who live with family or roommates, lack of privacy could be a barrier.
- Security: Use a HIPAA-compliant platform to safeguard client information.

Virtual therapy is my favorite option because it allows you to make an impact while maintaining flexibility. Personally, I've been able to serve clients in both Florida and New Jersey through my licensure and coach entrepreneurs globally, breaking geographical barriers.

It provides easy access to clients who could be ill, have transportation issues or geographical location limitations such as a snowstorm or rain. When these circumstances arise, clients don't have to cancel if virtual access is an option. This in turn provides more consistency and security for your practice. There's also less overhead cost.

One thing you do have to take into consideration is your licensing. You have to make sure that when you're providing therapeutic services to somebody that you are licensed in their state. Again, sometimes there are exceptions to that with COVID, but overall, this is something you always have to consider.

You additionally have to consider confidentiality: that there is a private, secure space on both sides of the screen. Most people live with other people. Be sure to assess whether your client is going to have the privacy and confidentiality they need to have a successful session.

The next consideration is HIPAA compliance. Again, you want to make sure that the platform that you're using protects their privacy. This is a legal necessity for private practice. Be sure to research the laws in your state and the states you are licensed in to assure HIPAA compliance.

Option 2: Professional Presence

A lot of the documentation that's required to start your private practice—establishing a business structure or applying for your license—is going to need a physical address and you don't want to use your home address, right? You want to protect your own confidentiality. Having a business address is a necessity, and many forms won't accept a P.O. box.

Look for services that provide a professional mailing address. Some services even provide a phone number and receptionist services. These setups are low-cost and help you establish credibility as you build your client base.

Option 3: Hourly Office Space

When I first started, I didn't even realize hourly office spaces existed, but they can be a game-changer. These spaces often offer a mailing address, phone-answering services, and flexible usage terms—ranging from hourly rates to monthly packages. Sometimes they will provide you a mailbox option as well, which comes in handy when you need to provide a professional address. You might be able to have a month to month contract; however, many places require more than that—six months or a year.

The pros are that you have a great cost-effective option when you're starting your practice and you're starting to schedule clients without a huge initial overhead. It also offers the professional presence and the office that people need in order to feel like you're a professional in the industry.

Some cons are that it does become expensive as you start seeing more clients per week. Also, the space that you use may not always be the same, and may sometimes be a conference room and not necessarily an office space, so that can feel a little awkward and unsettling for both you and your clients. Additionally, you're unable to decorate or personalize the space to your liking and you will also be shuffling files and personal items back and forth from home to the space you're using because typically there's no space for storage allowed.

Another con is that there's no office space for you to do notes. Because you're paying by the hour, if you have a break in between clients, you can't just stay in the space and do your notes. Additionally, if a client doesn't show for their scheduled session, you still have to pay for the space that you reserved, you can't just say "well, they didn't show."

Pros:

- Cost-effective when you're starting out.
- Offers a professional setting for sessions.

Cons:

- Costs can add up as your client load increases.
- Availability isn't guaranteed, which can disrupt consistency for you and your clients.
- Many spaces don't allow for storage or personalization, meaning you'll need to transport everything back and forth.
- You're responsible for the reserved time regardless of cancellations.

While hourly spaces can be a practical stepping stone, they may not feel stable enough for some practitioners.

Option 4: Shared/Subleased Space

Sharing a space with another clinician can strike the perfect balance between affordability and professionalism. You might sublease specific days or times that align with your schedule, such as evenings or weekends. This arrangement works well for practitioners with part-time hours or those balancing other responsibilities. This can be either set days of the week or a certain number of days per month. Some clinicians will choose to split-up days into daytimes and evenings. Whatever your scheduling needs are, it's likely that sharing an office space can balance out nicely.

If you don't need a space full-time, this option lowers your overhead cost. Usually, there is a flat fee per month or for a certain number of hours per month. For example, I'm using a shared space on Tuesdays and Thursdays for the entire month which costs $600. These agreements are created between the practitioners and vary based on needs.

Pros:

- Cheaper than a full-time lease.
- A consistent, professional office space.
- Opportunities to personalize the shared space and store supplies.

Cons:

- Scheduling limitations, as your access depends on the sublease agreement.
- Sharing the space may occasionally lead to conflicts or overlap.

I've seen this work beautifully for clinicians at different stages of their careers. There are many opportunities to find or create a situation that meets everyone's needs.

Option 5: Full-Time Private Office

Last but not least, you can have a full-time, dedicated, private space of your very own. Now the biggest pro of this is that it's completely flexible to your schedule. You can change your schedule, and schedule according to your client's preference. It offers the most flexibility, for you and your client, which is great when you're trying to create a thriving and fulfilling private practice on your terms. There's no concern with damage to your personal property because there's nobody else coming in and sharing the space. You're able to completely personalize the space because it's yours and you're not sharing it. It is the most cost effective when you have a steady clientele.

Things you do have to take into consideration is that there will probably be an annual lease, a contract you have to sign, most likely a security deposit, first month, and last month's rent. It's an empty space that you'll have to furnish so that's where some of the additional expenses come in—for example, a desk, chairs, couch, computer, decorations, lighting, supplies, printer, copier, etc. Also, depending on the lease, the renter may be responsible for utilities, painting, repairs, and other building costs. Consider what your budget is and take all of these costs into account when making your decision about having an office space.

Pros:

- Full control over your schedule.
- Ability to personalize the space to reflect your style and brand.
- Cost-effective in the long run for a thriving practice.

Cons:

- Higher upfront costs for furnishings and setup, including furniture, décor, and office equipment.

- Responsibility for additional expenses like utilities, repairs, and maintenance.

One last thing I want to mention—*location, location, location*—it matters. Consider the accessibility of the location. If you have a building with more than one floor, make sure that there's handicap parking, an elevator, and stairs. I recently had a new client who wouldn't schedule an initial session until he was assured there were stairs, because one of his fears was getting trapped in an elevator. You want to ensure that your clients are comfortable, feel safe, and that the setting you create is healing.

Make sure your location has what you need, such as a waiting room and a restroom. If your clients use public transportation, choose a location that's on the bus line. Take your time to consider all the factors and make the best decision for you and your clients.

Taking Action

Now it's decision time. Which option feels most aligned with your current stage of business? Maybe you've discovered options you hadn't considered before, or perhaps this has clarified what's next for you. Remember, your decision isn't set in stone—you can always adjust as your practice evolves.

Take a moment to reflect on your long-term goals. What do you envision for your practice? Write it down and start making moves toward the option that feels most comfortable right now. Progress is made one decision at a time, and you're already on your way.

Janessa Borges, LCSW

Lesson 4: In-Network or Out-of-Network

This is my personal favorite topic to discuss with new private practice owners thinking about opening their doors. It's time to decide whether you're going to participate with insurance panels (in-network), or decide to have a fullpaying, out of pocket private practice, also known as out-of-network. In this lesson, you'll learn all about insurance paneling, third-party insurance companies, as well as the pros and cons of each.

Employee Assistance Program (EAP)

An Employee Assistance Program (EAP) is a workplace benefit that provides employees with confidential support and resources to help them manage personal and work-related challenges. EAPs typically offer services such as counseling, mental health support, legal and financial advice, stress management, and assistance with family or substance abuse issues. These programs are designed to improve employee well-being, productivity, and overall job satisfaction while reducing workplace stress and absenteeism. EAP services are usually free for employees and their families and are provided by external professionals to ensure confidentiality.

This is a very important additional option to partnering with insurance panels. Different companies contract with separate third-party agencies. Companies essentially outsource different benefits for their employees, including behavioral health. Most clinics partner with EAP and insurances in order to have more referral streams.

Here are some cons to consider. Each EAP company has different, although similar, billing processes, so you're still billing and you're still responsible for all the paperwork necessary. EAP services typically have the lowest reimbursements. Also, some EAP clients are mandated by their employer due to insubordination, so they are not always willing participants. I have found that mandated individuals are often resistant, bitter, and angry, and personally, I'm in a place in my practice where I really love to work with people that want to willingly work with me and through their issues, so keep this in mind when you are considering EAPs.

I want to offer a few more considerations regarding EAPs. Although the patient has a zero dollar responsibility always, they do need to secure an authorization number prior to their session or it won't be covered. Some people will tell you that they already have the authorization number, and they'll be mailed documentation. However, if you do not have an authorization number, you will not be paid. Pro tip: I actually ask potential clients to provide me their authorization number, even though I know I don't need it to bill right away because the insurance company will be mailing me documentation. I always ask for that number and I make sure to tell them if they don't have that number before your session, the company will not pay for the session and the client will be financially responsible for that session.

Sometimes EAP benefits are provided by the patient's general insurance company or medical insurance; however, that's not always the case. The EAP generally covers a range from three to eight sessions. In the past, I've seen the average be three authorized sessions, and then you have to contact to provide an update with recommendations in order to receive an authorization for more sessions. Sometimes, six to eight sessions might be authorized in totality.

Insurance Paneling

Here are the facts, it typically takes 90 to 120 business days to become paneled with insurance companies. You have to apply to each individual insurance company separately to be credentialed. You need to locate the insurance panel you're interested in partnering with first. You look for "provider's option", "work with us", a "provider relations" or "contracting" and then you contact them to apply. It's typically done via electronic platforms, depending on the agency you're working with. The insurance company has a set fee schedule based on your degree, your credentials, your practice location—which includes region, state, and zip code—and the pre-existing needs for your type of provider, your location, or the type of services you provide.

If you move states, you have to reapply. Also of note, you don't get to determine or dictate your own fee schedule. Once you're offered a "package", you'll gain access to your fee schedule. You don't know how much they offer until after you apply. Some clinicians will talk to friends to get a sense of the pricing structure, however, insurance companies don't make their fee schedule public because they don't want people to start negotiating. It's often very challenging to find the fee schedule for a company, and once again, it varies depending on your expertise, your level, your degree, how long you've been working with them and your credentialing in general. Once you are paneled with insurance, you can request an increase, however, it's rarely considered.

It's important to note that it takes anywhere from 60 to 120 days to be pulled "out of network"—to end your contract with insurance panels. So, it takes almost as long to get out as it does to get in. Typically, by the time you're ready to pull out of the insurance company, you've made a pretty conscious decision; so it can be frustrating at this point to be tied to a contract.

I know of several clinicians who believe that if they tell a patient, "I'm not accepting your insurance anymore", they'll just have an understanding—or they'll have a patient sign a document acknowledging that the client is not agreeing to work with an insurance company—but that's not how that works. Please make sure that's not something you're doing. Pulling out of your contract with insurance panels is a process and requires documentation.

Real Talk

Clinicians usually partner with insurance because they are fearful of failing at their practice. They assume that insurance panels are the next step, the only step, or just what they have to do to succeed.

So, what's your reason forgoing "in network" with insurance panels—if you are planning to do that?

Just because you're contracting with insurance panels, doesn't guarantee your practice is going to be a success. You still need to learn how to market your practice. So yes, you'll be listed in a directory, but alongside hundreds—at times thousands—of other clinicians. You still have to know how to stand apart from the competition on that list.

Paneling with Insurance: Step-by-Step Guide and Detailed Pros and Cons

One of the biggest decisions you'll make as a private practice owner is whether to panel (also called credential) with insurance companies or operate as an out-of-network provider. This choice will shape the structure of your practice, impact your financial goals, and influence your work-life balance.

Let's break it down step by step and explore the advantages and challenges of each option so you can make an informed decision.

The Process of Paneling with Insurance

Paneling with insurance involves becoming an in-network provider for one or more insurance companies. Here's how the process works:

1. **Research Insurance Companies:** Start by identifying the insurance companies you want to work with. Consider the most

commonly used providers in your area and the types of clients they typically serve.

2. **Submit an Application:** Each insurance company has its own credentialing process. Applications often require:

- Proof of licensure and liability insurance.
- Copies of your business registration and tax documents.
- Your National Provider Identifier (NPI) and Employer Identification Number (EIN).
- A resume or CV detailing your professional experience.
- A completed W-9 form.

3. **Verification and Approval:** The insurance company will verify your credentials, review your application, and check for any disciplinary actions on your license. This process can take anywhere from 60 to 180 days.

4. Contract Negotiation: Once approved, you'll receive a contract outlining reimbursement rates for each type of session or service. Be prepared to negotiate if the rates seem too low to sustain your practice.

5. Set Up Billing: After signing the contract, you'll need to familiarize yourself with the insurance company's billing platform. This involves learning how to submit claims, track reimbursements, and handle denials or delays.

What Does Working with Insurance Look Like?

Once paneled, you'll take on additional administrative tasks:

- Insurance Verification: Before seeing a new client, you'll verify their insurance benefits to confirm coverage and identify any copays or deductibles.

- Claims Submission: After each session, you'll submit claims to the insurance company for reimbursement. Claims must be accurate, detailed, and compliant with insurance requirements.
- Payment Delays: Reimbursements are often delayed, ranging from two weeks to several months, depending on the company and the complexity of the claim.
- Missed Appointments: You won't be reimbursed for no-shows or late cancellations.

Pros of Paneling with Insurance

1. Increased Access for Clients: Insurance paneling allows clients to use their benefits, making therapy more affordable and accessible.

2. Steady Stream of Referrals: Many clients seek in-network providers to minimize

out-of-pocket expenses, leading to a higher number of inquiries and bookings.

3. Community Impact: Partnering with insurance helps ensure mental health services are accessible to underserved populations.

4. Built-In Marketing: Being listed in insurance directories increases your visibility, as potential clients often search for providers through their insurance networks.

Cons of Paneling with Insurance

1. Lower Reimbursement Rates: Insurance companies often set rates significantly lower than the standard private-pay fees, which means you'll need to see more clients to maintain your income goals.

2. Increased Administrative Work: You'll spend a considerable amount of time

verifying benefits, submitting claims, handling billing errors, and managing denied claims.

3. Delayed Payments: Insurance companies can take weeks—or even months—to reimburse you, creating cash flow challenges.

4. Limits on Services: Some insurance plans dictate the number of sessions a client can have or require pre-authorization for specific treatments.

5. Burnout Risk: The combination of a high caseload and lower income per session can lead to fatigue and emotional exhaustion.

Benefits of Going Out of Network

Opting out of insurance paneling doesn't mean you're excluding clients who use insurance. Instead, you'll be considered an "out-of-network" provider. Here's why many clinicians choose this route:

1. Higher Income Per Session: Without being tied to insurance rates, you can set your own fees that reflect your expertise and the value of your work.

2. Fewer Administrative Burdens: No more billing insurance, verifying coverage, or managing denied claims.

3. Flexibility in Care: You can offer services tailored to your clients' needs without being limited by insurance restrictions.

4. Improved Work-Life Balance: Seeing fewer clients for higher rates allows you to prioritize your well-being, avoid burnout, and spend more time with your family.

Addressing Common Concerns

I understand the hesitation some clinicians feel about stepping out of network. You may worry:

- "What if clients can't afford me?"
- "Am I being selfish by not accepting insurance?"

Let me assure you—choosing a business model that supports your health, family, and goals does not make you selfish. In fact, it allows you to show up as the best version of yourself for your clients.

To make your services more accessible, you can:

- Offer Sliding Scale Fees: Adjust your rates based on clients' financial situations.
- Provide Pro Bono Services: Dedicate a portion of your caseload to clients in need. For example, during the pandemic, I worked with a long-time client—who was furloughed—at no cost until she was back on her feet.

Practical Considerations

If you choose to panel with insurance, here are some tips to ensure a smooth experience:

- Stay Organized: Use practice management software to track claims, manage billing, and streamline administrative tasks.
- Know Your Limits: Monitor your caseload to avoid overworking and burning out.
- Communicate with Insurance Panels: If you become full or need to pause accepting new clients, update your status with the insurance companies promptly.

If you decide to go out of network, be transparent with your clients about costs and provide them with superbills to submit for potential reimbursement.

My Journey

For years, I struggled with the demands of being an in-network provider. Burnout was constant, and I felt like I was running on empty. When I finally made the decision to step out of network, everything changed. I regained control of my schedule, improved my quality of life, and still found ways to give back to my community.

Take Action

This is your business, and the decision to work with or without insurance is entirely yours. Review the information, reflect on your goals, and choose the path that aligns with your values. Whatever you decide, promise me one thing: Do not let fear guide your decision.

Ask yourself:

- What are my priorities for my practice and my life?

- Which model allows me to serve my clients while maintaining my well-being?

This is your journey, and you have the power to shape it however you see fit.

In the next chapter, we'll cover *Foundations 101*—including a checklist of everything you need to build a successful practice and a glossary of terms to navigate private practice and entrepreneurship with confidence.

Janessa Borges, LCSW

Chapter 2: Foundations 101

Lesson 1: Glossary of Private Practice Terms

This chapter is all about building your foundational knowledge with a glossary of essential private practice terms. Yes, it's a lot of information, but I've compiled the key terms you'll need to navigate the field confidently.

While I encourage you to pay attention as we go, give yourself grace. It's normal to feel a bit overwhelmed by the new acronyms and terminology. Remember, you can re-read this lesson, reference the PDF, and add to it as you grow. Let's jump in!

CAQH

You'll hear this term frequently: CAQH, short for the *Council for Affordable Quality Healthcare*. This centralized platform simplifies credentialing for healthcare providers. More than 900 health plans, hospitals, and organizations use CAQH to manage applications. If you're currently working in an agency or under someone else's clinical supervision, you may already have a CAQH profile. Be sure to check!

Consent for Release

Also known as a release of information, this document is essential for requesting, sharing, or discussing a patient's medical information. Even if other practitioners or hospitals already have a release on file, I recommend you request your own. It's a best practice to maintain updated records and ensure compliance with privacy standards.

Coinsurance vs. Copay

These terms often confuse clients—and sometimes even providers—so let's clarify:

Coinsurance: A percentage of the cost for a covered healthcare service, paid *after* the deductible is met. Example: If coinsurance is 20%, the client pays 20% of the bill, and insurance covers the rest.

Copay: A fixed amount paid for services or prescriptions, varying by treatment type. For example, a client might pay $25 per therapy session.

Understanding these differences is crucial when discussing coverage and payments with clients.

Deductible

The deductible is the amount a patient must pay out-of-pocket before their insurance begins covering costs. Deductibles vary widely by policy and can be a flat dollar amount or a percentage of the policy's coverage. Make sure to explain this to clients, as it often impacts their financial responsibility for services.

EAP

The Employee Assistance Program (EAP) supports employees dealing with personal or work-related challenges. Services typically include counseling, referrals, and follow-ups. Even if you're not working with EAP clients yet, it's helpful to familiarize yourself with the program and its processes.

Employer Identification Number (EIN)

The Employer Identification Number is a unique nine-digit number for business identification, similar to a Social Security number but used exclusively for business purposes.

You'll need an EIN to:

- Open a business bank account
- Apply for licenses
- File tax returns

Apply for an EIN early in your planning to avoid delays. While I discourage taking out loans to start a private practice, having an EIN in place ensures you're prepared for any necessary financing or operational requirements.

Employer Identification Number (EIN) and Tax ID are often used interchangeably, but there are some distinctions:

- EIN (Employer Identification Number): A unique nine-digit number issued by the IRS to businesses for tax filing and reporting purposes. It is used primarily by employers, corporations, partnerships, and other entities.
- Tax ID (Taxpayer Identification Number): A broader term that includes different types of identification numbers issued by the IRS, including:
  - EIN (Employer Identification Number) – for businesses.

- SSN (Social Security Number) – for individuals.
- ITIN (Individual Taxpayer Identification Number) – for non-U.S. residents and others who don't qualify for an SSN.

So, while an EIN is a type of Tax ID, not all Tax IDs are EINs.

HIPAA

The Health Insurance Portability and Accountability Act (HIPAA) of 1996 established standards for the privacy, security, and electronic exchange of health information. HIPAA compliance is critical in private practice and impacts how you:

- Handle patient confidentiality
- Use technology for virtual sessions
- Communicate with clients via email, phone, or messaging platforms

Ensure your processes and platforms are HIPAA-compliant to safeguard protected health information (PHI).

In-Network vs. Out-of-Network

In-Network: Contracted with an insurance panel. Providers sign agreements to offer services at negotiated rates, billing the insurance company directly.

Out-of-Network: Not contracted with insurance panels. Providers set their own rates and either accept private pay or help clients seek reimbursement from their insurance. This option offers greater flexibility but requires clients to pay upfront in most cases.

Personally, I prefer operating out-of-network and am a huge advocate for the freedom it provides; however, the choice depends on your business model and goals.

NPI

The National Provider Identifier (NPI) is a unique identification number for healthcare providers. Required under HIPAA, the NPI ensures efficient electronic transactions and is essential for billing and credentialing. Think of it as your professional ID as a therapist. If you're interning or newly licensed, your agency may handle this, but you'll need one when operating independently.

Out-of-Pocket Maximum

The out-of-pocket max is the cap on what a client pays for deductibles, coinsurance, and copays within a policy period. Once reached, the insurance covers 100% of eligible costs. Knowing this term helps you explain coverage to clients, especially those with high medical expenses.

This glossary is just the beginning. As you move through this book and beyond, you'll encounter these terms frequently. Don't stress about memorizing everything right now—you have this chapter as your go-to reference. Let's keep building your private practice foundation!

Janessa Borges, LCSW

Lesson 2: Private Practice Requirement Checklist

This chapter is all about the steps you need to take, presented as a checklist. But before we dive in, I'll walk you through each item and explain why it matters.

Some steps need to be completed before you move on to the next, while others can be skipped depending on your specific situation. However, the order I've laid out is intentional, so stick with me—we're building your foundation one step at a time.

Step 1: Your Clinical License

If you're planning to open a therapeutic private practice, your clinical license is non-negotiable in nearly every state. Some states made temporary exceptions during the pandemic, but those are rare. Since licensing laws vary, I strongly encourage you to verify your state's requirements.

For example, if you're a social worker, check with the National Association of Social Workers (NASW), both the national and local chapters. Getting clear on this upfront is essential, especially after all the time and effort you've invested in your education and training. You don't want to run into legal or professional issues later.

Step 2: Malpractice Insurance

Malpractice insurance is a must-have, even as a student or intern. It's not just about protecting yourself—it's about peace of mind. The cost is minimal when you're starting out and increases slightly as your practice grows. The key benefit? Coverage is retroactive, starting from the moment you first enroll.

When I was an intern, I made it a priority to get malpractice insurance, even though I wasn't required to. Why? Because I'm all about doing things ethically, legally, and with a clear conscience. Whether you're working for an agency, completing your clinical hours, or opening your practice, this is a step you don't want to skip.

Step 3: Your NPI Number

If you're a clinician, you probably already have an NPI (National Provider Identifier) number. It's essentially your unique identifier as a healthcare professional. If you've worked for an agency, your NPI might already exist, even if you weren't actively using it.

When I applied for mine, I discovered I already had one tied to the nonprofit I was working for at the time. To avoid confusion, check whether you already have an NPI number. The link in your checklist will help you verify or apply for one if needed.

Step 4: Your Tax Identification Number

While your NPI number identifies you as a clinician, your Tax Identification Number (TIN) identifies your business. These two numbers serve different purposes, but both are essential. To apply for your TIN, use the link I've provided in the checklist. Choose the business name you've decided on, and make sure you're consistent with how you register it across all platforms.

Step 5: Registering Your Business

Once you have your TIN, you'll need to register your business. Start by registering it in your state, then check if your city, town, or county requires additional registrations.

For example, in Florida, I had to register my practice name with the state, city, and county where my office is located. These registrations often come with associated fees, sometimes called business or county tax receipts. It's essentially the cost of legally conducting business in your area.

Step 6: CAQH Credentialing

If you plan to accept insurance, you'll need to create a profile with CAQH (Council for Affordable Quality Healthcare). Think of CAQH as a centralized application system for credentialing with insurance companies. It's like FAFSA for financial aid or the LSAC platform for law school applications.

Through CAQH, insurance companies can verify your malpractice insurance, licensing, and other credentials. You'll need to keep your profile updated and re-attest periodically to ensure compliance. This step streamlines the process of becoming in-network with insurance providers.

If you are in private practice and plan to accept insurance or work with third-party payers, you typically need to be registered with CAQH. CAQH ProView is a centralized database used by insurance companies to credential healthcare providers, ensuring they meet the necessary qualifications to be reimbursed for services.

However, if you run a fully cash-pay practice and do not bill insurance, CAQH registration is not required.

When You Need CAQH:

- If you're contracting with insurance companies for reimbursement.
- If you want to be in-network with health insurance plans.
- If you're required by a hospital or group practice that participates in insurance.

When You Don't Need CAQH:

- If your practice is 100% private pay (self-pay clients only).
- If you do not plan to accept insurance, Medicare, or Medicaid.

- Even if you don't need CAQH now, it can be useful to have a profile in case you decide to take insurance in the future.

Step 7: Open a Business Checking Account

Now for the exciting part—opening your business checking account! This is a major milestone that makes your business feel official. Before heading to the bank, ensure you have your TIN, business registration documents, and any other required paperwork.

Pro Tip: While you're at the bank, open a business savings account, too. You might be thinking, "Why would I need a savings account if I'm just starting out?" Here's why: As soon as you begin earning money, you'll want to set aside funds for taxes, emergencies, or future growth. It's a small step now that can save you a lot of headaches later.

This checklist is designed to guide you through the foundational steps of launching your private practice. By following this order, you'll be equipped with the essentials to confidently move forward. Take it one step at a time, use the cheat sheet for support, and remember—you're building something amazing.

Chapter 3: Administration of Private Practice

Lesson 1: Startup Costs of Private Practice

Now that we've laid the groundwork—covering the four key decisions, foundational needs, and checklist steps to get started—it's time to dive into the nuts and bolts of administration.

In this chapter, we'll focus on one of the biggest questions new practitioners face: What does it really cost to start a private practice?

Here's the truth: You don't need as much as you think you do.

Many aspiring practitioners stall their dreams because they're overwhelmed by the perceived financial demands or convinced they need every tool, gadget, and professional service before they can even begin. My goal in this lesson is to show you what's truly essential, what can wait, and how to start smart without overspending.

The Essentials: Needs vs. Wants

When starting your private practice, focus on needs—the absolute necessities that ensure you can legally, ethically, and responsibly serve your clients. Everything else falls into the "nice-to-have" category. Let's break it down.

What You Need to Begin

1. An Office or Virtual Platform

If you're meeting clients in person, you'll need a space—whether it's a full-time office, a shared hourly setup, or a subleased location. If you're working virtually, ensure your platform is HIPAA-compliant. (We covered this in detail in a previous module, so revisit it if needed.)

2. A Professional Business Line

Clients need a reliable way to contact you. Avoid generic voicemails or juggling personal calls with professional ones. There are affordable options to set up a business line, and remember—this is a deductible business expense. Check with your accountant for specifics.

3. Malpractice Insurance

This is non-negotiable. Malpractice insurance protects you, your clients, and your practice. I recommend opting for the highest coverage you can afford. Policies typically start around $150 per year and can retroactively cover you from the moment you sign. Trust me, this peace of mind is worth every penny.

4. Your License and Continuing Education

To practice legally, you must maintain your professional license and fulfill your state's continuing education (CEU) requirements. Remember to budget for license renewal fees and ongoing training every two years.

5. Your Tax ID and Business Registration

Your Tax ID enables you to get paid, and registering your business with your city or county ensures you're operating legally.

The Bare Bones: Start Simple

At its core, all you truly need to begin is your education, training, a professional space (virtual or physical), and the tools to operate ethically and legally. Fancy extras? They can wait.

Here are some common "wants" that you might feel tempted to prioritize but don't actually need to get started:

1. Fancy Stationery

While customized stationery feels professional, it's unnecessary when you're just starting out. A well-designed PDF template on quality paper does the trick.

2. A Secretary

In the early stages, you're likely wearing all the hats. Answering phones, scheduling clients, and verifying insurance might seem overwhelming, but these tasks are manageable until your practice grows.

3. Expensive Furniture

If you're renting an office, check if furniture is included. Otherwise, start with the basics: a desk, a comfortable chair, and seating for your clients. Look for budget-friendly options and upgrade later.

4. Thousands of Business Cards

Keep it simple—order 250-500 professional cards. Your contact details may change as your business evolves, so avoid overstocking and wasting money on updates.

5. A Website

Yes, a professional website is important, but a simple one page scrolling website to provide a professional presence will do just fine for now. Keep it simple. On my podcast and YOUtube channel, my own web designer and I guide you through cost-effective alternatives and share bonus tips from my own web designer to help you avoid common pitfalls.

Where to Save, DIY, and Delegate

- Save: Look for free or low-cost resources to keep startup costs down.
- DIY: Templates for invoices, intake forms, and even basic branding are easy to create on platforms like Canva.
- Delegate: When you're ready, consider outsourcing tasks that drain your time and energy, like bookkeeping or phone answering.

A Personal Note

When I started my private practice over 14 years ago, I didn't have the perfect office, an admin team, or fancy business cards. What I did have was determination, a plan, and a deep desire to help my clients. Over the years, I've learned how to grow without breaking the bank—and I want you to start smarter than I did.

Remember: Every successful practice starts with a dream, but it's the practical steps that bring it to life. Stick to what you need, stay focused, and trust that you can build the rest as you grow.

What's Next?

In the next lesson, we'll explore how to make smart financial decisions that set you apart and position your practice for long-term success. I'll share strategies to scale your income, provide top-tier care for your clients, and create a fulfilling life for yourself—all while staying true to your values and vision.

Janessa Borges, LCSW

Lesson 2: Initial Paperwork

This chapter is all about the critical documents you'll need when starting your practice and working with new clients. Proper documentation ensures a smooth and professional experience for both you and your clients, setting the tone for effective and ethical care.

Intake Documentation: Your First Impression

The intake paperwork is your starting point. This set of documents not only gathers critical client information but also serves as the foundation for your professional relationship. This is the bare minimum of what you should have in place and ready prior to advertising your services. Always double-check with your state, board, and attorney.

Here's what it includes:

1. Client Demographic Information

>What It Is: Basic information about your client, including their legal name, contact details, date of birth, and emergency contact information.
>
>Why You Need It: This ensures you have accurate records for communication, billing, and emergency purposes.
>
>What It Should Contain:
>
>- Full legal name
>- Address, phone number, and email
>- Date of birth
>- Emergency contact (including name, relationship, and phone number)
>- If applicable, referral source (e.g., doctor, friend, or online search)

2. Insurance Information

What It Is: Details about your client's health insurance provider, policy number, and group number.

Why You Need It: Whether you accept insurance or provide out-of-network reimbursement documentation, this information is essential.

What It Should Contain:

- Insurance provider's name and phone number
- Policy and group numbers
- Subscriber details (if different from the client)
- A copy of the insurance card (front and back)

3. Emergency Contact Form

What It Is: A form identifying someone to contact in case of an emergency.

Why You Need It: It's a safety measure and provides insight into your client's support system.

What It Should Contain: Name, relationship to the client, and multiple contact numbers.

Legal and Administrative Documents

4. HIPAA Notice of Privacy Practices

What It Is: A document informing clients about their rights under the Health Insurance Portability and Accountability Act (HIPAA).

Why You Need It: It's legally required and ensures clients understand how their personal health information is used and protected.

What It Should Contain:

- Explanation of client privacy rights

- How their information may be used or shared
- Contact information for privacy-related questions or complaints

5. Consent to Treat Form

What It Is: A form where clients provide written consent to receive services.

Why You Need It: This is a legal safeguard ensuring clients understand and agree to treatment.

What It Should Contain:
- Nature and scope of services
- Limits of confidentiality
- Acknowledgment of voluntary participation
- Space for client signature and date

6. Practice Policies Agreement

What It Is: A comprehensive document outlining your practice's policies.

Why You Need It: To set clear expectations and avoid misunderstandings.

What It Should Contain:

- Office hours and communication guidelines
- Cancellation policy (e.g., fees for no-shows or late cancellations)
- Fees for services, including payment methods and billing procedures
- Boundaries around social media and dual relationships
- Policy on terminating treatment

7. Good Faith Estimate

What It Is: A document providing an estimate of the expected costs of services.

Why You Need It: Compliance with the No Surprises Act, which protects clients from unexpected charges.

What It Should Contain:
- Expected session frequency
- Estimated costs for an agreed-upon treatment plan
- Disclaimers about potential changes

Clinical Documents

8. Medical and Mental Health History

What It Is: A form collecting information about a client's physical and mental health background.

Why You Need It: To provide context for treatment and identify potential risks or co-occurring conditions.

What It Should Contain:

- Medical diagnoses and history of treatment
- Current medications and prescribing physicians
- Previous therapy experiences
- Family mental health history

9. Suicide Risk Screening Form

What It Is: A tool to assess a client's risk of self-harm or suicidal ideation.

Why You Need It: To address safety concerns proactively and implement appropriate interventions if necessary.

What It Should Contain:

- Direct questions about thoughts of self-harm
- History of suicide attempts
- Current emotional state and stressors
- Emergency plan if risk is identified

Streamlining the Process

Gone are the days of paper-heavy practices. Modern practice management software allows you to digitize these documents, making intake efficient and secure. Digital forms offer:

- Convenience: Clients can complete forms at their own pace before their first session.
- Security: Compliance with HIPAA standards for data protection.
- Efficiency: Automatically integrates with client records, saving time for you and your staff.

Action Steps

1. Audit Your Current Documentation: Make a list of what you have and identify gaps.
2. Create or Update Forms: Ensure they reflect the specific needs of your practice.

3. Consult an Expert: Have an attorney review your contracts and policies for legal compliance.
4. Digitize Your Process: Use a practice management system to simplify workflows.
5. Set a Review Schedule: Periodically revisit your documents to ensure they remain relevant and up to date.

One of the most common questions I receive is, "What if the client didn't complete the paperwork?" My answer is "No ticket, no laundry." Your clinical documentation is your legal protection. It is your permission to treat your client, consistent with all of your practice policies. I know what it feels like when you're starting off. When I started I used to have spare forms in my office. If a client didn't have it ready: I would hand it to them before we began, I would leave it in the waiting room, I would email it to them. I would also remind them that in preparation for their session to kindly complete the documentation as thoroughly as possible because this would allow me to start focusing on their goals instead of on paperwork, making the most of our first session. Feel free to do the same for your practice. If you use electronic forms, do the same:

"If you can please take a moment to look for your email, log in and complete the forms before we get started."

I also blame my attorney for the legal paperwork and requirements.

Final Thoughts

Your paperwork reflects the professionalism of your practice. Clear, comprehensive, and client-centered documentation ensures that you're not only meeting legal and ethical standards but also creating a welcoming and organized environment for your clients. Start with the essentials, refine as you go, and remember—clarity leads to confidence, which sets the foundation for success. Don't copy someone else's intake paperwork, make sure you have your own set that is reviewed by an attorney as soon as possible. Yes, it's an expense; however, not having the proper documentation can cost more in the long run—financially, professionally, and emotionally.

Lesson 3: Everything Admin—Building a Strong Foundation

This chapter is filled with the nitty-gritty details that keep your practice running smoothly. I've packed a lot into this chapter, so let's get started!

Scheduling: The Heartbeat of Your Practice

Most patients prefer speaking to someone directly to schedule their appointments, which is why having a dedicated phone line is critical. That said, I'm a huge fan of electronic scheduling. For my practice, I use SimplePractice for both billing and scheduling, and it has truly been a game-changer. *Visit janessaborges.com/simplepractice for my* affiliate link to receive a free month to try it out.

SimplePractice makes everything seamless, and after trying several platforms, it's my clear favorite. It's user-friendly, reliable, and incredibly versatile. As a bonus, I've arranged a special promotion for you—it's included in the support resource document. You'll find a discount code there if you want to give it a try. That said, choose what feels best for you. Your system needs to align with your style and workflow.

Security: Protecting Your Practice and Clients

Security is non-negotiable in private practice. Every system you use—whether for documents, intake forms, contracts, or credit card processing—must be secure. Here's how to ensure you're safeguarding sensitive information:

- Use a dedicated, secure computer: Avoid sharing it with others.
- Lock access to your files: Physical file cabinets should have number or key locks, and digital platforms should offer reliable backup systems.

- Verify platform security: Ensure your chosen platform meets confidentiality standards and is HIPAA-compliant.

Confidentiality isn't just a policy—it's a promise. Whether it's your email, phone, or documents, you're responsible for honoring your clients' trust while protecting your own boundaries.

Reminders: Let Technology Do the Heavy Lifting

Gone are the days when I personally called patients to remind them of appointments. Now, with SimplePractice, clients can schedule through my website and automatically receive reminders—48 hours in advance. This feature has saved me so much time and ensures that I'm not left waiting in my office for no-shows.

Communication: Balancing Access and Boundaries

Clear communication is crucial, but so are healthy boundaries. Let's break it down:

1. Email: Use a secure email system that only you can access.
2. Portal Messages: Many platforms, including SimplePractice, offer secure messaging. I like this option because it's HIPAA-compliant, and all communications are logged and timestamped. I keep portal messages strictly to scheduling or re-scheduling sessions.
3. Text Messages: Personally, I don't allow clients to text me. While my business line is a cell phone, I've set up an auto-reply informing clients that messages aren't monitored and directing them to email or call instead. This ensures clarity, accountability, and security.

Voicemail: Professional and Confidential

Your voicemail is often the first impression of your practice. Keep it professional and succinct, emphasizing confidentiality.

Setting Boundaries: Protecting Your Energy and Practice

From day one, it's essential to establish clear, healthy boundaries. These aren't just for your benefit—they protect your clients, too. Communicate your policies upfront and make them part of your practice's standard operating procedures (SOP).

Here's an example:

If a client calls with a "quick question," it's rarely quick. I encourage clients to email me instead. This creates a written record and allows me to respond thoughtfully. My typical response?

"Thank you for reaching out. If you need to reschedule, let me know. Otherwise, please jot

down your concerns, and we'll address them during your next session."

For urgent matters, I offer the option to schedule a phone session. This approach sets expectations and maintains boundaries while ensuring clients feel supported.

Your Practice, Your Rules

Remember, this is *your* business. You have the authority to create policies that align with your values and adjust them as you grow. Take a moment now to reflect:

- What feels fair and comfortable for you?
- What policies will help you serve your clients effectively while honoring your needs?

Write these down and implement them as part of your SOP.

Final Thoughts: Own Your Role as a Leader

You're not just a therapist—you're a business owner and leader. Establishing boundaries, creating policies, and leveraging the right tools will set the tone for a thriving practice.

As always, I'll leave you with some tough love: *You are the professional. You set the standard.* If you don't define your boundaries, no one else will.

Janessa Borges, LCSW

Lesson 4: Billing Made Simple

As promised in the administrative section of your journey, we're diving into billing—an essential yet often intimidating part of running your private practice.

We're going to start off focusing on the Health Care Financing Administration Form (HCFA 1500) also known as the Centers for Medicare and Medicaid Services (CMS) 1500 Health Insurance Claim Form.

This is the standardized billing document you'll encounter that's used by healthcare providers in order to bill insurance companies and streamline claims for medical services. It's crucial to understand how it works, even if you're not handling every detail yourself.

When I started my practice, I had no guidance, no roadmap, and certainly no training on billing. I vividly remember sitting at Starbucks, staring at a stack of HCFA forms I'd picked up at Office Depot, completely unsure of where to start. I'd spend hours on weekends filling out each form by hand—yes, by hand—patient by patient. It was tedious, overwhelming, and, looking back, entirely unnecessary. But at the time, I didn't know better, and there were no accessible resources like this one to help me navigate the administrative side of private practice.

Fast forward to today: We've come a long way. Technology and tools now make this process so much simpler, but I still believe it's essential to understand the basics. Whether you're working in-network or out-of-network, knowing how the HCFA form works empowers you to troubleshoot, assist clients, and ensure accurate billing.

A Quick Note for Out-of-Network Providers

If you've decided to go fully out-of-network, congratulations! The HCFA form may not be a regular part of your workflow. However, it's still helpful to know how it works, as some clients might request assistance submitting claims to their insurance for reimbursement.

Let's Break It Down: Box by Box

We're going to walk through the HCFA 1500 form step by step. This might seem overwhelming at first, but trust me, it'll all make sense by the end.

Boxes 1-3: Identifying the Insurance

The first section is where you'll indicate the type of insurance: Medicare, Medicaid, TRICARE (military), Champ VA (for veterans), or Other. For most private practices, you'll likely select "Other."

Next, enter the patient's insurance ID number, which can be found on their insurance card. Then fill in the patient's name (last, first, middle initial) and date of birth. Be careful here—details matter, and small errors can lead to claim rejections.

Boxes 4-7: Patient vs. Insured Information
Here's where it can get a bit tricky. Often, the patient and the insured are not the same person. For example, if your client is a child, the insured might be a parent. Pay close attention to this section and double-check that you've entered the correct names, addresses, and relationships (e.g., "Self," "Spouse," or "Child").

Box 9: Secondary Insurance
If the client has secondary insurance, you'll need to complete this section. For simplicity, if there's no secondary insurance, you can leave this blank.

Box 10: Reason for Visit

Indicate whether the visit is related to employment, an auto accident, or another reason. For most therapy practices, this will typically be "No."

Boxes 11-13: Insurance Policy and Group Numbers

Refer to the client's insurance card for this information. On the left side of the form, enter the client's information; on the right, enter the policyholder's details if they're not the same person. This distinction is important for claims processing.

Boxes 14-24: Service Details

Now we get into the nitty-gritty: the dates of service, diagnosis codes, and procedure codes. This section requires precision, as insurance companies rely on these details to process claims correctly.

Use your ICD-10 and DSM-5 for diagnosis codes and CPT codes for services:

- 90791: Initial assessment
- 90837: 50-minute session
- 90834: 45-minute session
- 90832: 30-minute session

You'll also include your NPI (National Provider Identifier) number and indicate the place of service (e.g., "office").

Box 25 and Beyond: Signatures and Submission
For signatures, I now use "signature on file," which is much more efficient than having patients sign every single form. Ensure your documentation includes a copy of their original signature. When entering dates, use the date the form was completed or the date of service.

Lessons Learned

When I started, I thought I was clever by photocopying pre-filled sections of the form to save time. It worked temporarily but wasn't a sustainable system. Thankfully, we now have billing software that automates much of this process. However, understanding the basics is invaluable, especially when you're starting with only a few clients and handling billing yourself.

My Favorite Billing Strategy

If you're ready to invest in tools, I highly recommend exploring electronic billing platforms. They simplify the entire process, reduce errors, and free up your time to focus on what you do best: helping clients. But even if you're not ready to make that leap, mastering the HCFA form ensures you're prepared and confident.

Final Thoughts

Billing might not be the most glamorous part of running a private practice, but it's one of the most critical. By understanding the HCFA form and the overall billing process, you'll avoid common pitfalls, streamline your operations, and provide better service to your clients. Remember, every successful private practice starts with mastering the fundamentals—and this is one of them.

Lesson 5: Mastering Invoices & Superbills

In this chapter, we'll dive into the essential tools you'll need for managing invoices and superbills in your private practice. By the end, you'll have a clear understanding of what these documents are, how to create them efficiently, and how to avoid the mistakes I made when starting out.

Let's start by reviewing the basics. Earlier, we talked about HCFA forms and their role in billing. Now, I want to introduce you to the tools I use to streamline my practice. As I mentioned earlier, I love *SimplePractice*. It's my go-to platform for managing everything: from scheduling and billing, to sending reminders and storing documentation. It's my one-stop shop, and it's saved me countless hours.

When I first started, I did everything by hand. I used to write invoices manually, create Word documents, and handle client requests one by one. Looking back, it was tedious and inefficient. But you're not going to make those same mistakes. In this chapter, I'll walk you through how to create invoices and super bills using a software system, step by step.

What Is an Invoice?

An invoice is a record of services rendered and the amount owed for those services. Whether you use a software system like *SimplePractice* or another tool, the elements are the same. Let me show you how I create an invoice for a mock client.

Here's what an invoice typically includes:

- Practice information: Your name, address, phone number, and email.
- Client information: Their name, address, and, if applicable, details about their relationship to the insured (e.g., spouse or child).

- Service details: The date of service, the CPT code (in this example, 90837 for a 50-minute session), and the service fee (e.g., $200).
- Billing information: Your Tax ID, NPI number, and a breakdown of charges, payments, and the balance.

Once generated, the invoice can be printed, downloaded, or emailed directly to the client. Simple, right?

What Is a Superbill?

A superbill is slightly more detailed than an invoice. It's used by clients to request reimbursement from their insurance provider for out-of-network services. I always charge my clients at the time of their session and have my system generate a super bill monthly.

Here's what a super bill includes:

- Practice information: As listed on the invoice.
- Client details: Name, date of birth, and insurance information (if available).
- Provider information: Your name, NPI number, phone number, email, and license details. If you're licensed in multiple states, include all relevant license numbers.
- Service and diagnosis details: The CPT code (e.g., 90837), diagnosis code (e.g., F43.20 for Adjustment Disorder, Unspecified), date of service, number of units, and service fee.

The superbill also needs to state that it's for insurance reimbursement. Once generated, it's up to the client to submit it to their insurance company, along with any additional forms required by their insurer.

What Is a Client Statement?

Finally, a client statement provides an overview of all transactions and sessions. It's essentially a detailed financial record, showing:

- Previous balances (if any).
- A chronological list of sessions, charges, and payments.
- The current balance.

This document is helpful for clients who need a comprehensive breakdown of their account history.

Why I Recommend SimplePractice

I've used a variety of billing systems over the years, but *SimplePractice* stands out. It integrates seamlessly with my calendar, allows clients to schedule through the portal, and generates invoices, superbills, and reports with just a few clicks. It even sends automated appointment reminders, reducing no-shows and improving efficiency.

For me, the cost of the platform is more than worth it. *Visit* janessaborges.com/simplepractice *for my* affiliate link to receive a free trial to try it out.

Lessons Learned

Looking back, I can't believe I used to do all of this manually. It was time-consuming and it left so much room for error. Today, I rely on systems that not only save time but also ensure accuracy and professionalism.

As you build your private practice, remember this: your time is valuable. Invest in tools and systems that allow you to focus on what truly matters—helping your clients.

What's Next

Congratulations, Rockstar! You did it! I hope you have your business structure and your business name all set and that you have all the bells and whistles that you need to get started—now that you know that you don't need all the bells and whistles you thought you needed to open your doors.

You've now completed Private Practice Blueprint® 101. You understand the foundation: the essential components that you need to get your practice up and running and to start getting clients.

When you're ready to market and grow your practice, my complete Private Practice Blueprint® program, will take you through all of the marketing pieces: how to stand apart from the competition, how to market your practice, how to become visible, how to have a successful private practice opening with a wait list, and how to avoid burnout and overwhelm. And later on, when you're ready, how to scale your practice—because there truly is a limit to the one-on-one work you're able to do. Just visit janessaborges.com/therapists for all the details and a free masterclass. I'm so excited for you, I am always rooting for you, and most of all, I can't wait to see your private practice and hear about all your successes.

I hope that all of your dreams come true.

www.ingramcontent.com/pod-product-compliance
Lightning Source LLC
Chambersburg PA
CBHW060512030426
42337CB00015B/1868